COLOMBIA

ECUADOR

Equator 0°

N

W • E

S

4°S

PACIFIC OCEAN

Cape Negra

• Piura

Chiclayo •

Trujillo •

Chimbote •

8°S

PERU

ANDES MOUNTAINS

Callao •
Lima ✪

Ica •

Iquitos •

Putumayo River

Amazon River

Marañón River

Huallaga River

Ucayali River

Pucallpa •

BRAZIL

Purús River

Urubamba River

Apurímac River

Madre de Dios River

Cuzco •

BOLIVIA

Lake Titicaca

Arequipa •

16°S

0   150   300 Miles
|——|——|——|——|——|——|
0   150   300 Kilometers
Oblique Conic Conformal Projection

CHILE

80°W   76°W   72°W   68°W

Discovering
South
America

PERU

Discovering South America

PERU

Charles J. Shields

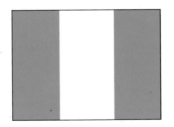

Mason Crest Publishers
Philadelphia

Produced by OTTN Publishing, Stockton, N.J.

Mason Crest Publishers
370 Reed Road
Broomall, PA 19008
www.masoncrest.com

First printing

1 3 5 7 9 8 6 4 2

Library of Congress Cataloging-in-Publication Data

Shields, Charles J., 1951-
  Peru / Charles J. Shields.
       p. cm. — (Discovering South America)
Summary: Presents information on the geography, history, economy, and people of Peru.
Includes a chronology, recipes, project ideas, and more.
Includes bibliographical references and index.
  ISBN 1-59084-288-X
1. Peru—Juvenile literature. [1. Peru.] I. Title. II. Series.
  F3408.5 .S55 2003
  985—dc21
                                      2002011899

Table of Contents

Discovering South America

James D. Henderson

South America is a cornucopia of natural resources, a treasure house of ecological variety. It is also a continent of striking human diversity and geographic extremes. Yet in spite of that, most South Americans share a set of cultural similarities. Most of the continent's inhabitants are properly termed "Latin" Americans. This means that they speak a Romance language (one closely related to Latin), particularly Spanish or Portuguese. It means, too, that most practice Roman Catholicism and share the Mediterranean cultural patterns brought by the Spanish and Portuguese who settled the continent over five centuries ago.

Still, it is never hard to spot departures from these cultural norms. Bolivia, Peru, and Ecuador, for example, have significant Indian populations who speak their own languages and follow their own customs. In Paraguay the main Indian language, Guaraní, is accepted as official along with Spanish. Nor are all South Americans Catholics. Today Protestantism is making steady gains, while in Brazil many citizens practice African religions right along with Catholicism and Protestantism.

South America is a lightly populated continent, having just 6 percent of the world's people. It is also the world's most tropical continent, for a larger percentage of its land falls between the tropics of Cancer and Capricorn than is the case with any other continent. The world's driest desert is there, the Atacama in northern Chile, where no one has ever seen a drop of rain fall. And the world's wettest place is there too, the Chocó region of Colombia, along that country's border with Panama. There it rains almost every day. South America also has some of the world's highest mountains, the Andes,

The green countryside of Peru.

and its greatest river, the Amazon.

So welcome to South America! Through this colorfully illustrated series of books you will travel through 12 countries, from giant Brazil to small Suriname. On your way you will learn about the geography, the history, the economy, and the people of each one. Geared to the needs of teachers and students, each volume contains book and web sources for further study, a chronology, project and report ideas, and even recipes of tasty and easy-to-prepare dishes popular in the countries studied. Each volume describes the country's national holidays and the cities and towns where they are held. And each book is indexed.

You are embarking on a voyage of discovery that will take you to lands not so far away, but as interesting and exotic as any in the world.

(Opposite) Machu Picchu, the ancient Peruvian city located in the Andes, was once an Inca fortress. Though the power of the Incas was destroyed by Spanish invaders during the 16th century, Peru today still has a strong native culture. (Right) The town of Pevas on the Río Ampiyacu, in the Amazon River basin.

1 Land of Contrasts

PERU IS A LAND of great contrasts. It has lush tropical *rain forests*, coastal deserts, and soaring mountains.

Located in the west-central part of South America, Peru shares borders with Chile (to the south), Bolivia and Brazil (to the east), and Colombia and Ecuador (to the north). Peru's 496,223 square miles (1,285,220 square kilometers) of territory make it slightly more than three times the size of California. In South America, only Brazil and Argentina are larger.

From north to south, Peru is 1,554 miles (2,501 km) long. It has three natural regions—the *costa*, or coast; the *sierra*, or Andean highlands; and the jungle or rain forest region east of the Andes.

The Dry Coast

The coastal region accounts for 11 percent of Peru's territory. It's a narrow strip only 12 to 62 miles (19 to 100 km) wide. The altitude varies from sea level to 3,281 feet (1,001 meters). Although the coastal strip is mainly arid, seasonal rains occur in the north—especially during a weather pattern known as El Niño. El Niño occurs every three to seven years when unusually warm ocean conditions appear along the western coast of South America. During El Niño, the wet weather conditions off Peru and Ecuador move east, bringing heavy rains that can cause extensive flooding.

Usually, however, the Peruvian coast receives less than two inches (5 centimeters) of rain each year. This is because most of the moisture carried by the eastern *trade winds* falls on the *cordilleras*. But many of Peru's 52 valleys are *arable*. They are farmed using a combination of ancient Indian irrigation methods and modern technologies. In addition, warm, foggy clouds known as *garúa* shroud many of the foothills of the sierra from June to October, providing enough moisture to support grasslands.

The *costa* has been the home of important Peruvian civilizations for many centuries. Among the famous Indian sites archaeologists have unearthed are Chan-Chan, Nazca, and Sipan. Today, the *costa* is the center of Peru's industrial, commercial, and agricultural activity. Lima, the political and economic capital, is located here, with its more than 7 million inhabitants.

Along the coastal plain temperatures normally average about 68°F (20°C) throughout the year. The climate is moderated by winds blowing from the cold offshore current known as the Peru Current (also called the Humboldt Current).

The Chilly Sierras

Peru's sierra, or Andean highland, region ranges from 52 to 155 miles (84 to 249 km) wide and covers 30 percent of the country's territory. The Andes Mountains run through Peru north to south, separating the Pacific coast in the west from the Amazon Basin rain forest in the east. In Peru the Andes divide into two major systems: the Cordillera Occidental (western) and the Cordillera Oriental (eastern). The Peruvian Andes boast 174 snow-capped peaks over 16,000 feet (4,880 meters) high. Thirty-nine peaks rise above 19,600 feet (5,978 meters) high. The highest of all is Huascarán, at 22,205 feet (6,768 meters). That's more than 4 miles (6 km) in the air! At that elevation the climate is arctic.

A Peruvian woman with her child.

The llama is an animal native to South America. These creatures, which can grow to more than six feet tall and weigh over 400 pounds, have been domesticated for more than 4,000 years.

Below the peaks, the altiplanos, or high plateaus—12,500 to 14,100 feet (3,813 to 4,301 meters) above sea level—end abruptly at the edge of deep canyons carved by the Apurímac, Cotahuasi, and Colca Rivers. In southeastern Peru, on the border with Bolivia, lies the world's highest *navigable* lake, Titicaca. The lake, at about 12,500 feet (3,813 meters) above sea level, contains more than 40 islands and is rimmed by important archaeological sites and beautiful Spanish colonial towns.

In the sierra region, the temperature ranges during the year from about 20°F to 70°F (-7°C to 21°C). Precipitation is usually limited, because parts of the sierra rise above the rain clouds. But in some lower areas, heavy rains fall from October to April. In the southeastern sierra, for example, annual rainfall averages 32 inches (81 cm). The eastern slopes of the Andes receive more than 100 inches (254 cm) of rain annually because storm systems stall against the towering mountainsides. Runoff feeds major rivers and fast-flowing streams, about 50 of which start in the sierra and descend steeply to the coastal plain.

The Humid Jungle

East of the sierra and extending to the borders with Ecuador, Colombia, Brazil, and Bolivia lies Peru's largest natural region—the jungle. Covering some 59 percent of the country, this region—which is often referred to by the somewhat confusing name *la montaña*, meaning "mountain"—consists of two distinct subregions: the lowland and highland jungles.

The lowland jungle, by far the larger of the two, is a tropical rain forest lying between 250 and 1,300 feet (76 and 396 meters) above sea level. In northeastern Peru, the Ucayali and Marañón Rivers—both more than 1,000 miles (1,609 km) long—come together at the start of the mighty Amazon River, which flows east across Peru into Brazil. In the vast Amazon Basin, temperatures can be quite hot, and average annual rainfall can reach up to 150 inches (381 cm). This rain, which falls primarily from November through April, supports dense, lush vegetation. The Amazon Basin is also crisscrossed by a network of rivers and streams. In addition to the Amazon, Ucayali, and Marañón, major rivers that flow through this region include the Napo, Tigre, and Pastaza, all of which rise in Ecuador. The Putumayo River forms the border between Colombia and Peru.

The highland jungle, located on the eastern foothills of the Cordillera

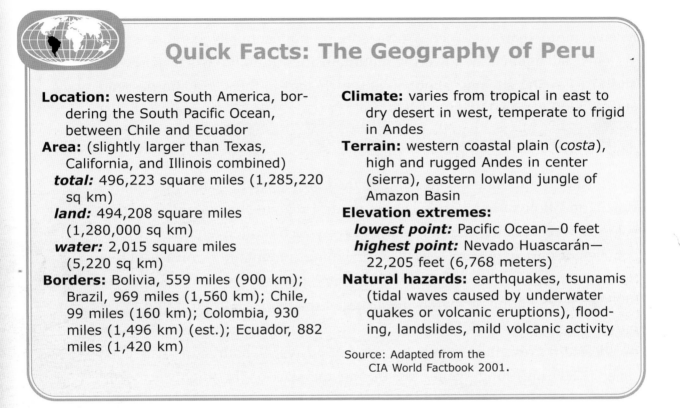

Quick Facts: The Geography of Peru

Location: western South America, bordering the South Pacific Ocean, between Chile and Ecuador

Area: (slightly larger than Texas, California, and Illinois combined)
 total: 496,223 square miles (1,285,220 sq km)
 land: 494,208 square miles (1,280,000 sq km)
 water: 2,015 square miles (5,220 sq km)

Borders: Bolivia, 559 miles (900 km); Brazil, 969 miles (1,560 km); Chile, 99 miles (160 km); Colombia, 930 miles (1,496 km) (est.); Ecuador, 882 miles (1,420 km)

Climate: varies from tropical in east to dry desert in west, temperate to frigid in Andes

Terrain: western coastal plain (*costa*), high and rugged Andes in center (*sierra*), eastern lowland jungle of Amazon Basin

Elevation extremes:
 lowest point: Pacific Ocean—0 feet
 highest point: Nevado Huascarán—22,205 feet (6,768 meters)

Natural hazards: earthquakes, tsunamis (tidal waves caused by underwater quakes or volcanic eruptions), flooding, landslides, mild volcanic activity

Source: Adapted from the
CIA World Factbook 2001.

Oriental at altitudes between 1,600 and 9,200 feet (488 and 2,806 meters), is a thin band between the Andean highlands and the lowland jungle. This densely forested area is known locally as *la ceja de selva* ("the eyebrow of the jungle"). Though wet and humid like the lowland tropical rain forest, the highland jungle enjoys a *temperate* climate and features an unusual ecosystem—the cloud forest. Cloud forests are evergreen forests that are almost permanently shrouded in mist because the cooler temperatures on mountain slopes cause moisture to condense and form clouds.

Colorful Plants and Animals of Peru

The plant life of the jungle, the sierra, and the coastal plain varies widely. The vast, fertile rain forests contain a rich profusion of trees, plants, and jungle vines. There you'll find mahogany, cedar, rubber, and cinchona trees; sarsaparilla and vanilla plants; and a variety of exotic tropical flowers. Other tropical and subtropical plants with commercial significance that

Latex drips out of a rubber tree. Trees such as this flourish in hot, moist climates like those of Peru and Brazil, providing about 99 percent of all natural rubber. To collect the latex, tappers cut grooves in the bark of the tree with a sharp curved knife. At the bottom of the groove, they place a metal spout. The latex oozes out of the cut into the spout, collecting in a small cup.

Peruvians have a tradition of craftsmanship. This gold figure of an Inca warrior can be found in a museum in Lima.

grow in this region include coffee, tea, cocoa, pineapple, banana, and citrus fruits. Animals of the rain forest include the jaguar, cougar, armadillo, peccary, tapir, anteater, several dozen species of monkey, alligator, turtle, and a variety of snakes and insects. Among the birds are the parrot, the flamingo, and other tropical species.

Only hardy plants can survive in the rugged sierra, and even then not at the highest altitudes. Sierra vegetation, which is adapted to surviving on very little water, includes mesquite, eucalyptus, cactus, and shrubs and grasses. A few grazing animals can handle the rough terrain and sparse rainfall here. They include the llama, vicuña, chinchilla, and guanaco.

Peru's *arid* coastal plain supports mainly desert vegetation, such as shrubs, grasses, and tuberous plants. Its wildlife, similarly limited, includes little other than lizards, insects, tarantulas, and scorpions, although shorebirds such as gulls and terns do make this area home.

On the other hand, Peru's Pacific waters are rich in anchovy, pilchard, haddock, sole, mackerel, smelt, flounder, lobster, shrimp, and other marine species. Lake Titicaca and other bodies of water in the sierras teem with fish as well.

Peru's birds include the giant condor, and species of robin, phoebe, flycatcher, finch, partridge, duck, and goose.

Que es saco de las tinieblas asu admirable luz

MAYTA CAPAC INGA IV.

CAPAC YVPANCVI ING

El Melancolico Conquistô a los Charcas El Avariento descubrio y atesoro hasta el famoso Cerro de Potosí Hizo el ce de riquezas Conquistô a los Ayma lebre Puente de Apurimac para sus con y Qtuchuas y otras Provincias del quistas Tuvo 50 Hijos Vivio 120 años rra y Valles. Mando ǧ le entierr la Coya fue Mama Chimbo Yachi Vrma con sus joyas Vivio 140 años La Sucediole su Hijo Mama Chimbo Cahua sucediole su H

(Opposite) This painting of Inca rulers was done by a Spanish artist in Cuzco after the region had fallen under the control of Spain. (Right) The conquistador Francisco Pizarro led an army of fewer than 200 men against thousands of Inca warriors, but by capturing the Inca ruler he was able to conquer the empire.

2 A Rich, Turbulent History

PERU IS THE cradle of some of South America's most advanced Indian civilizations. These include the renowned Inca, who dominated the central Andean region when the Spanish arrived in the early 16th century.

The first inhabitants of Peru were nomadic hunter-gatherers who lived in caves in Peru's coastal regions. The oldest known site, Pikimachay, may date to 18,000 B.C., some archaeologists believe.

By about 4000 B.C. people in the area had begun cultivating food crops. Eventually the growing of such crops as beans, squash, chili peppers, corn, and potatoes would enable the establishment of large settlements and the creation of sophisticated cultures. By 1200 B.C. a culture know as the Chavín, known for its well-crafted pottery, textiles, and stone carvings, had arisen in the northern highlands of Peru. Its influence would last until around 300 B.C.

Over the centuries several other cultures, including the Salinar, Nazca, Wari, Mochica, Chimú, and Tiahuanaco, flourished.

The Rise and Fall of the Inca Empire

Around A.D. 1200 the Inca, a people of the Peruvian highlands, established themselves at Cuzco. For several hundred years they remained there. Then, in the early 1400s, the Inca began conquering neighboring tribes. By midcentury they had established a large empire, which would eventually stretch from parts of modern-day Colombia and Ecuador in the north to central Chile and northwestern Argentina in the south.

The Inca were fierce, disciplined warriors, as one would expect for a people who managed to conquer so much territory in a relatively brief time. But only careful, capable, and—when necessary—ruthless administration held their vast empire together. The Inca built a remarkable system of roads for rapid communication and the movement of soldiers. They encouraged conquered tribes to adopt Inca culture, often by educating the other tribes' nobles, but any attempts to rebel were brutally crushed. At the top of Inca government and society stood the Sapa Inca, or emperor, who had absolute authority over all his subjects. Below him the empire was administered by officials responsible for 10,000, 5,000, 1,000, and 500 adult males. Below them were foremen responsible for groups of 50 and 10. Imperial spies made sure all the officials were doing their jobs and alerted the authorities to possible trouble within the realm. The system worked with incredible efficiency for about a century.

In 1531, however, a 180-man Spanish expedition set sail from

Panama, bound for Peru. That expedition, commanded by an aging *conquistador* named Francisco Pizarro, would eventually bring the Inca Empire to its knees.

From the Inca coastal city of Tumbes, in what is today northernmost Peru, the Spaniards set out for the interior on May 13, 1532. The march proved grueling, though Pizarro and his men met with no opposition from the Inca—probably because they had let it be known that they only wanted to pay their respects to the emperor, Atahuallpa. Finally, in mid-November, they encountered Atahuallpa at Cajamarca. Undeterred by the presence of roughly 50,000 Inca warriors in the area, Pizarro planned to take bold—and treacherous—action. He arranged for a meeting with Atahuallpa in Cajamarca's square. There, on November 16, the Spaniards launched a surprise attack, firing their cannons, charging the Inca warriors, and seizing the emperor. With their horses, their armor, their guns, and their steel swords, the Spaniards slaughtered thousands of the lightly armed Inca warriors, who fled in chaos under the onslaught.

Because all authority had traditionally channeled up to the emperor, the Inca people found it difficult to organize effective resistance to the invaders after Atahuallpa's capture. For his part, Atahuallpa attempted to bargain with Pizarro, offering to gather a roomful of gold in exchange for his freedom. Pizarro failed to live up to his end of the bargain. In 1533, after the promised treasure had poured in from throughout the empire, the Spaniards executed Atahuallpa.

The early years of Spanish settlement in Peru were chaotic. The Spaniards abused the Indians horribly, forcing the conquered peoples to toil on Spanish estates or working them to death by the thousands in silver mines. An uprising by Manco Capac, an Inca ruler installed by Pizarro, flared in 1536. Meanwhile, rival conquistadors fought among themselves for the spoils of Peru. After defeating and killing Diego de Almagro, a former partner, Pizarro himself was killed by Almagro supporters in 1541. Worst of all, from the point of view of Spain, some colonists even resisted the authority of the Spanish crown.

Eventually, though, Spain brought order to the unruly colony, making it the center of Spanish rule in South America. In 1542, Spain established the Viceroyalty of Peru, which until the 18th century included Panama and all of Spanish South America except Venezuela. Lima, which had been founded by Pizarro in 1535, became the viceroyalty's capital.

Though Spanish Peru prospered—by the 17th century it had become the second-largest producer of silver in the world—the Indians remained poor and oppressed. In 1780 an Indian billing himself as the new Inca savior took the name Tupac Amaru II and led an uprising of Peru's Indians. By the following year, however, the rebellion had been put down, and most of the leaders were rounded up and executed.

The Rise of Independent Peru

Peru remained under Spanish control until 1821, when the Argentinian-born general José de San Martín—a hero of the South American wars of independence from Spain—entered Lima and proclaimed Peruvian independence on July 28. But Peru's liberation wasn't ensured until two 1824 victories over Spanish royalists: the Battle of Junín, won by General Simón

Bolívar in August, and the Battle of Ayacucho, won by General Antonio José de Sucre in December.

A long period of instability followed. Peru was governed by a series of generals who tried to increase Peru's influence in South America. A short union with Bolivia (1836–39) disintegrated. In 1866, Peru won a brief war with Spain but was later humiliated by Chile in the War of the Pacific (1879–83), at the conclusion of which Peru was forced to surrender profitable nitrate fields in the northern Atacama Desert. A border dispute between Peru and Chile simmered until the signing of a temporary treaty in 1929.

Peru also went to war with Ecuador over a border dispute in 1941. Border conflicts erupted again in early 1981 and early 1995. In 1998 the governments of both countries signed a peace treaty, which finally established the border. In late 1999, the govern-

A Peruvian man holds a portrait of Tupac Amaru, an 18th-century native leader who claimed to be descended from the last Inca chieftain. In 1780—81 he led an unsuccessful Indian revolt.

Simón Bolívar (1783–1830) is one of the most famous figures in South America's history. Bolívar's victory over the Spanish at the Battle of Junín in August 1824 helped ensure Peru's freedom.

ments of Peru and Chile agreed to the last outstanding article of their 1929 border agreement, too.

Economic and Political Contests

In the late 19th century, a new railway connected the mines of the highlands with the ports of the coast. Foreign investors poured money into the project, bringing major economic improvements to Peru.

With the improvements in the economy, however, came a power struggle. The upper class, composed of whites of European descent—called criollos, or Creoles—resisted attempts at social and economic reform demanded by the lower, non-European classes. During the first half of the 20th century, Peru had 18 presidents. Five were removed from office, and four resigned. Many were dictators who used force to maintain control of the country.

Adding to the government's difficulties was a population explosion in the mid-20th century. The total population almost tripled from more than 7 million in 1950 to nearly 20 million in 1985. At the same time, a great wave of out-migration swept the sierra. From about 1950 to 1975, Peru was transformed from a *rural* to an *urban* society as people relocated from the countryside to the cities in search of work. By 1980, more than 60 percent of Peru's workforce was located in towns and cities, principally the capital, Lima (containing one-third of the total population), and the coast (containing three-fifths).

This major population shift resulted in urban poverty. Peru's economy was unable to expand fast enough to provide work for newcomers. In 1985 half of Lima's nearly 7 million inhabitants lived in shacks on the edge of the city, and at least half of the country's population was unemployed or underemployed.

In 1965, a *guerrilla* group calling itself the National Liberation Army used weapons supplied by Cuba to launch attacks on the government. In the 1980s, a series of nationwide labor strikes and bloody attacks in the countryside by the *Communist* Shining Path guerrillas caused severe political instability. Another guerrilla group, the Tupac Amaru Revolutionary Movement (MRTA), also gained strength during this period. Anti-government forces profited from the sale of illegally grown coca, which is used to make cocaine.

In 1990, when Alberto Fujimori won the presidential election, many Peruvians hoped he could bring an end to the guerrilla violence. But another, equally dangerous threat to the stability of Peru existed: continued unemployment, poverty, and high *inflation*. Fujimori took drastic steps that

Alejandro Toledo gestures after being sworn in as president of Peru on July 28, 2001, in Lima. Toledo was Peru's first freely elected president of Indian descent. He promised to govern in the interests of the nation's poor majority.

caused inflation to drop from 7,650 percent in 1990 to 139 percent by 1991. Faced with opposition to his reform efforts, he dissolved Congress on April 4, 1992. He then revised the constitution, called new congressional elections, and continued major economic overhauls, including putting state-owned companies into private hands.

After the Shining Path had apparently been smashed, Fujimori was reelected in April 1995. But his decision to break with the constitution and seek a third term in 2000 brought more political and economic turmoil. Amid widespread allegations of voting fraud, Fujimori won the election.

Just weeks after he had begun his third term as president, a bribery and human rights scandal broke. When the taint of wrongdoing reached him, Fujimori fled the country and resigned from office in November 2000. A caretaker government presided over by Valentín Paniagua Corazao took on the responsibility of conducting new presidential and congressional elections, in April 2001.

Alejandro Toledo, an economist and Andean Indian, won the presidency. In his inaugural address in July 2001, Toledo listed among his priorities strengthening democratic institutions, fighting corruption, and reducing poverty and unemployment by improving Peru's economy.

(Opposite) A vegetable vendor displays her wares. Many Peruvians are poor farmers who live off the crops they produce and sell any surpluses for extra money. (Right) Peruvian currency. The country has the seventh-largest economy in Latin America, although most of Peru's people have a lower standard of living than people in other countries of the region.

3 A Divided Economy

WHERE ITS ECONOMY is concerned, Peru resembles two different nations. On the coastal plain, a modern economy exists that is built on trade, agriculture, manufacturing, and services. In the Andes, however, descendants of the Inca and other Indians scratch out meager livings through *subsistence farming*, with few of the amenities of modern life.

The International Monetary Fund estimated Peru's 2001 *gross domestic product (GDP)*—the total value of goods and services the country produced—at $52.9 billion. In overall size, Peru's economy ranked seventh among Latin American nations. Yet in terms of GDP per capita—a measure of each citizen's share of the wealth generated by the economy—Peru ranked 12th among Latin American countries.

29

Peru is largely a land of impoverished farmers and barely employed workers who live in shacks. According to a census taken in the mid-1990s, about 1 in 5 Peruvians is an unskilled worker; about as many are low-skilled farm laborers. Even inside Lima, the capital city, 50 percent of workers provide only simple services. This includes selling inexpensive items in the street, or driving unlicensed taxis, for example. When former president Alberto Fujimori took drastic steps to bring down inflation in the early 1990s, hundreds of thousands of Peruvians were thrown out of work. A key step in Fujimori's program was ending government-funded jobs.

Throughout Peru, only a fraction of workers earn good wages. Almost half of Peruvians live below the poverty line. The poorest fifth of the population earns less than 5 percent of the national income average of $4,500. And in Peru one's economic prospects are largely tied to ancestry: since the colonial days, a white *elite* has enjoyed most of the wealth generated by Peru's economy, while the Amerindian population has suffered great poverty.

In September 2001 President Alejandro Toledo announced a new program called *A Trabajar* (To Work). This program aimed to create 400,000 jobs in its first two years. Most of the funding for *A Trabajar* comes from foreign aid. The United States contributed more than $1.3 billion in aid to Peru between 1990 and 2000, which included food and disaster relief.

A Fragile Economy

Although Peru's economy depends heavily on agriculture, the mining and fishing industries are becoming more important. In good years, about three-fourths of Peru's trade with other nations comes from exports such as

A security guard stands in front of bags of drugs seized in Peru over a 10-month period during 2000. The bags of cocaine, marijuana, opium, and heroin were incinerated.

cotton, coffee, sugarcane, minerals, oil, and fish meal. Unfortunately, this is a limited range of products. When their prices drop on the world market, or harsh weather ruins Peru's crops, a shock wave runs throughout Peru's economy. The chief export markets are the United States, Japan, the United Kingdom, China, and Germany. Peru's leading imports include electrical and electronic items, foodstuffs, metals, chemicals, and transportation equipment.

About one-fifth of Peru's workforce is engaged in farming, forestry, or fishing. Most of the farms along the coast raise crops for export—sugarcane, potatoes, rice, corn, cotton, and wheat. Llamas, sheep, and vicuñas provide wool, hides, and skins. Many of the farms in Peru are small and limited to subsistence crops. To earn an income, some farmers raise coca, from which the drug cocaine is refined.

Forests cover about half of Peru. Forest products include balsa lumber and balata gum, rubber, and a variety of medicinal plants. The cinchona tree in Peru yields quinine, first introduced to Europe by Peruvian Catholic missionaries around 1640. Quinine reduces high fever from malaria and helps stop painful muscle cramping. Peru's Indians rely on many other local plants for their healing properties, and biochemists around the world are investigating the possibility of developing medicines from plants growing in Peru.

In 1994 Peru became the world's second-largest fishing nation after China. It is also the world's leading producer of fish meal. In 2000, Peru produced 60 percent of the world's fish meal, used mainly in farm animal and pet feed. Three-fifths of the Peruvian catch is anchovies, used in fish meal. But in 1998, when the warming effects of El Niño on the South Pacific drove anchovies off Peru's coast to colder waters, this part of Peru's economy suffered greatly. The price of fish meal can also soar or drop depending on the global prices for soybean, the other main source of animal feed.

Peru ranks as one of the world's leading producers of copper, silver, lead, and zinc. Petroleum, natural gas, iron ore, molybdenum, tungsten, and gold are extracted in large amounts, as well.

Manufacturing is a small part of Peru's economy, but a number of modern

Quick Facts: The Economy of Peru

Gross domestic product (GDP*):
   $52.9 billion
GDP per capita: $1,923
Inflation: 1.5%
Natural resources: copper, silver, gold, petroleum, timber, fish, iron ore, coal, phosphate, potash, hydropower
Agriculture (10% of GDP): coffee, cotton, sugarcane, rice, wheat, potatoes, plantains, coca; poultry, beef, dairy products, wool; fish
Services (55% of GDP): tourism, banking, government services
Industry (35% of GDP): mining of metals, petroleum, fishing, textiles, clothing, food processing, cement, auto assembly, steel, shipbuilding, metal fabrication

Foreign trade:
   Exports—$7.3 billion: fish and fish products, copper, zinc, gold, crude petroleum and byproducts, lead, coffee, sugar, cotton.
   Imports—$7.4 billion: electrical and electronic items, foodstuffs, metals, chemicals, and transportation equipment.
Currency exchange rate 3.6762 nuevo sol = U.S. $1 (Aug. 12, 2002)

* GDP = the total value of goods and services produced in a year.
All figures are 2001 estimates unless otherwise noted.
Sources: CIA World Factbook 2002; International Monetary Fund.

industries have sprung up along the country's Pacific coast since the 1950s. Small factories turn out textiles, clothing, food products, and handicrafts. Items produced in large modern plants include steel, refined petroleum, chemicals, processed minerals, and fish meal.

Transportation

Peru's towering mountains make getting goods to market difficult. In 1999 Peru had about 45,298 miles (72,898 km) of roads, only 13 percent of which were paved. The main transportation route is a section of the

Peruvians paddle a dugout canoe down the river.

Pan-American Highway, which cuts through Peru from Ecuador to Chile, covering a distance of about 1,550 miles (2,494 km). Peru also has about 1,051 miles (1,691 km) of railroads. One trans-Andean line, the Central Railroad, climbs to 3 miles (nearly 5 km) above sea level, the highest point reached by any standard-gauge line in the world.

The most important inland waterway through Peru is the Amazon River, which can be traveled by ships from the Atlantic Ocean to the city of Iquitos. The 3,200-square-mile (8,288-sq-km) Lake Titicaca also serves as a waterway, with regular ship traffic between Puno, Peru, and Guaqui, Bolivia. Leading Peruvian seaports include Callao, Salaverry, Pacasmayo, Paita, and San Juan. The country's main international airports are located near Lima, Cuzco, Iquitos, and Arequipa.

The U.S.-Peru Connection

U.S. investment and tourism in Peru have grown gradually in recent years. U.S. exports to Peru totaled $2.4 billion in 2000, accounting for about 30 percent of Peru's imports. In the same year, Peru exported $2 billion in goods to the United States, accounting for about 30 percent of

Peru's exports to the world.

About 200,000 U.S. citizens visit Peru annually for business, tourism, and study. About 10,000 Americans live in Peru, and more than 400 U.S. companies have offices there.

A Yagua Indian man touches the beard of a scientist visiting the man's village in the Amazon rain forest of Peru. The indigenous Yagua exist by fishing, hunting, and living off the land.

(Opposite) Native children in the Amazon Basin. Amerindians make up about 45 percent of Peru's population. (Right) These colonial homes in Cuzco date from the early 19th century. Cuzco was once the center of the Inca civilization.

4 Two Peoples, Two Cultures

PERUVIAN CULTURE today reflects the influences of two major groups: Amerindians and Spanish. Six centuries of coexistence between these groups has produced a blending of their cultures. Yet in certain respects many of Peru's Indians still live apart from the rest of society, maintaining ancient traditions and ways of life.

Almost half of Peru's 27.4 million people are Indian. A large proportion of these Indians live in the highlands, where they continue to speak Quechua (the language of the Inca) and follow the traditions of their ancestors. Education here is limited, and poverty widespread. Indians who migrate to the cities for better opportunities generally work as servants or street vendors.

About 15 percent of Peruvians claim unmixed white descent. These

Quick Facts: The People of Peru

Population: 27,483,864

Ethnic groups: Amerindian, 45%; mestizo (mixed Amerindian and white), 37%; white, 15%; black, Japanese, Chinese, and other, 3%

Age structure:
0—14 years: 34.41%
15—64 years: 60.8%
65 years and over: 4.79%

Population growth rate: 1.7%

Birth rate: 23.9 births/1,000 population

Death rate: 5.78 deaths/1,000 population

Infant mortality rate: 39.39 deaths/1,000 live births

Life expectancy at birth:
total population: 70.3 years
male: 67.9 years
female: 72.81 years

Total fertility rate: 2.96 children born/woman

Religions: Roman Catholic, 90%; others (including Protestant and Evangelical), 10%

Languages: Spanish (official), Quechua (official), Aymara

Literacy rate (age 15 and older who can read and write): 88.7% (1995 est.)

All figures are 2001 estimates except where otherwise indicated. Source: CIA World Factbook 2001.

people, who tend to live in the coastal cities, are among Peru's best-educated and wealthiest citizens. They also enjoy the highest social status. In general, the more European a person looks, the greater his or her social standing.

Nearly 4 in 10 Peruvians are *mestizos* (of mixed Indian and white ancestry). Their status and economic positions tend to fall somewhere between those of whites and Indians. Mestizos make up a large percentage of middle- and lower-middle-class urban workers such as laborers, teachers, military personnel, and medical and legal workers.

Although 70 percent of Peruvians speak Spanish, dozens of *indigenous* languages, such as Quechua (the Incan language) and Aymara, continue to be spoken by Indians in the highlands. In remote parts of the Amazon, Spanish is rarely heard.

About 90 percent of Peruvians are Roman Catholics. The Indians, while outwardly Catholic, often blend Catholicism with traditional beliefs.

Basic public education in Peru is free and required for all children between the ages of 6 and 12. The *literacy* rate in Peru doubled in the second half of the 20th century, rising from 42 percent in 1940 to 89 percent in 1995. But many children in rural areas and the highlands do not attend secondary schools because there are none nearby. Similarly, many children of the urban poor stop going to school at age 12, because they must work to help support their families.

Folk performers, who imitate the traditional rituals of the ancient Indians, often use seashell horns in their performances.

Rich Traditions

During *pre-Columbian* times, Peru was one of the major centers of artistry in America. Pre-Inca cultures, such as Chavín, Paracas, Nazca, Chimú, and Tiahuanaco, developed high-quality pottery, textiles, and sculpture.

Drawing upon earlier cultures, the Inca continued to practice these crafts but reached even more impressive achievements. The Inca were a highly organized people, skilled in engineering, weaving, farming, the working of gold and silver, and the building of roads and towns. The mountain town of Machu Picchu and the buildings in Cuzco are excellent examples of Inca architecture and stonework. Inca builders used large stones of irregular sizes and, without mortar, fit the stones together so precisely that a sheet of paper could not fit between them. Cuzco was once the Inca capital, noted for its woodcarvings, sculpture, furniture, and paintings. Tourists today can visit amazing archaeological sites that display the abilities of the Inca people.

During the colonial period from the 16th to the 19th centuries, Spanish culture fused with the rich Inca tradition. In the Andes, the Spanish often built directly on top of Inca ruins. The Spanish introduced their version of urban planning, with cities laid out in checkerboard fashion. At first, their mansions, churches, and monasteries imitated Spanish renaissance art. Over time, however, these Old World styles showed signs of Indian influence, leading to new styles known as *mestizo* and *creole*. Initially colonial painting in Peru also imitated European painting, but as local artists grew more confident, a new and distinctive style developed. Artists turned their attention away from the real world and concentrated instead on Indian legends and fairy tales. Art was also strongly influenced by the Roman Catholic Church.

A tray of *cuy* (guinea pig) and potatoes is placed in a restaurant oven in Pisac.

The first Peruvian writer of renown was Garcilaso de la Vega, the son of a Spanish soldier and an Inca princess. In 1609 he published *Comentarios Reales de los Incas* (Royal Commentaries of the Incas), a vivid historical account of the Inca Empire and its culture. More recently, Mario Vargas Llosa has won worldwide acclaim for his novels and essays.

The Incas were lovers of music. Instruments such as the reed *quena* (flute), the *antara* (panpipe), conch shells, and the ocarina continue to be heard in Peruvian music. The Incas were also lovers of dance accompanied by song. Some popular folksongs and dances have survived the centuries, such as the *yariví*, a love song; the *huayno*, a rapid dance of the highlands; and the *cashua*, a circle dance.

African Influences

The Spanish brought African slaves to Peru in the 16th century to work in the gold and silver mines of the high Andes. The altitude and the brutal conditions killed them by the hundreds. Their masters sent others to work in the milder climate of the coast, where they labored on large haciendas, or private farms. It was in their small huts and in the sugarcane fields that Afro-Peruvian music and dance was born. These centuries-old forms gained renewed recognition in Peru about 40 years ago. The *Marinera* is an intricate and elegant dance of courtship accompanied by guitar, *cajon* (a wooden box), accordion, and handclapping by onlookers. Other important Afro-Peruvian rhythmic styles include the *Lando*, which comes from an African fertility dance, and the *Festejo*, which is a celebratory song and dance.

Spicy Food

Typical Peruvian dishes are spicy and vary depending on the location. Seafood is best on the coast, while the traditional Incan delicacy, roast guinea pig, can be sampled in the highlands.

(Opposite) Two young boys in Cuzco, which today is Peru's ninth-largest city. (Right) Farmers in Urubamba, a valley once sacred to the Incas. Most farmers in Peru struggle to survive.

5 The Highlands and Cities of Peru

EVER SINCE THE Spanish colonization of Peru, Andean communities have suffered from the breakdown of their pre-Columbian systems of farming. The Inca built extensive and highly productive irrigation networks and *terraces* called *andenes*. But over the centuries the land engineering fell into disrepair, in part because the Indians had to work for the Spanish rather than maintain their own fields. Today Andean Indians toil extremely hard to produce the meager amount of food and trade goods that sustain their families and villages.

The peasant family begins its day at dawn with chores such as tending animals, cutting firewood, and fetching water. Field work begins with a long walk to the often distant *chacras*, or small farms, which may be located at a different altitude from home and require several hours to reach. Where *chacras* are very far, farmers keep huts in which to store tools or stay for several days. Andean peasants of all ages and both sexes lead strenuous lives, hustling about steep pathways while carrying heavy loads.

Andean Indians repair, invent, and adapt most of their tools. They also prepare food from grain they have harvested and animals they have raised and butchered. Fifty percent of rural households have no appliances such as radios and TVs because there is no electricity, or the items are too expensive.

Burros are the most common beasts of burden in most of the highlands, because they are less expensive to take care of than horses or mules. Llamas and alpacas also are commonly used in the central and southern Andes, where they are still widely used for transport, wool, and meat. Peasant women and girls spin wool for hours. The wool is then sold to local artisans, who weave it by hand into clothing, blankets, and ponchos.

Family members and neighbors depend heavily on one another. They work side-by-side, celebrate successes, and share misfortune. But in villages where everyone knows everyone else, or knows about them, disagreements and feuds tend to be common. Village life can be difficult when conflicts erupt. The Peruvians have a saying: *"Pueblo chico, infierno grande"*—Small town, big hell.

Many young people tire of village life and migrate to the cities along the coast. When they leave, their loss as helpers cuts deeply into their families and communities.

In Peru, educational and employment opportunities are concentrated in and around the coastal cities. Many of these cities date from colonial times and boast interesting cultural attractions. Here are descriptions of some of the most interesting and significant cities in Peru:

Lima

Peru's capital, cultural and business center, and largest city is located in the heart of the country along the Pacific coast. Lima, also known as "the City of Kings," was founded by conquistador Francisco Pizarro in 1535 on the banks of the Rímac River. It became the center for the Spanish viceroyalty's business and administrative activities in the 16th and 17th centuries and one of Latin America's largest cities. Lima's location and wealth attracted numerous merchants, as well as pirates who attacked and plundered the city during colonial times.

In downtown Lima, the Plaza de Armas, regarded as the city's hub, boasts a 17th-century bronze fountain. Surrounding the plaza are three of the

A hillside shantytown on the outskirts of Lima.

city's most important structures from colonial times: the Catedral (cathedral) de Lima; the Palacio de Gobierno, also known as La Casa de Pizarro because it was once the conquistador's residence; and Lima's City Hall. The plaza was the scene of San Martín's proclamation of independence on July 28, 1821, marking the beginning of the end of Spanish colonial rule in Peru.

Several Lima museums display and preserve Peru's rich past. The most notable is the internationally famed National Museum of Anthropology and Archaeology.

Lima began to grow rapidly in the 20th century. Migration from the highlands and jungle became massive during the 1950s and later. People

A volcano rises over Arequipa, Peru's second-largest city.

went to the coast in search of better living opportunities. A belt of poverty formed around the old city, creating "microcities" or shantytowns. Lima's population today is more than 7 million.

Arequipa

Nicknamed "Ciudad Blanca" (White City) because most of its buildings were constructed of a white volcanic stone called *sillar*, Arequipa sits at an elevation of 7,600 feet (2,318 meters). Now Peru's second-largest city, it was founded by the Spanish on August 15, 1540, on the site of a ruined Inca town. Earthquakes leveled much of the city in 1687 and again in 1868.

Nearby mountains—including the volcanoes El Misti, Chachani, and Picchu Picchu—offer stunning vistas. Attractions within Arequipa include the beautiful colonial-era cathedral and the huge Convent of Santa Catalina, built in 1580 as a virtual city within a city. Arequipa also enjoys a dry, springlike climate year-round.

Cajamarca

The town of Cajamarca, located about 370 miles (595 km) northwest of Lima, is one of Peru's most historically significant places. Human settlement at Cajamarca goes back some 3,000 years. Between A.D. 500 and 1000 it flourished as a center of the Caxamarca culture. Around 1450, Capac Yupanqui, brother of the ruling Inca emperor Pachacutec, conquered Cajamarca and added it to the Inca Empire.

Cajamarca's expansive Plaza de Armas was built over the smaller square where, on November 16, 1532, Atahuallpa and his Inca warriors came face to face with the Spanish conquistadors led by Francisco Pizarro—with tragic results for the Inca. Visitors to Cajamarca can also see "el Cuarto del Rescate," the room Atahuallpa offered to fill with gold in exchange for his freedom. It measures about 22 feet (6.7 meters) by 17 feet (5.2 meters) and is 8 feet (2.4 meters) high.

Cuzco

No city combines Inca and colonial Spanish architecture more masterfully than Cuzco (also spelled Cusco and Qosqo). Nestled high in the Andes about 350 miles (563 km) southeast of Lima, this city of 290,000 inhabitants was once the capital of the Inca Empire, and the extraordinary stonework of the Inca is still very much in evidence. Cuzco also boasts many elegant Spanish churches, convents, and red-roofed colonial houses.

For all the city's charm, however, what makes Cuzco one of the most popular tourist destinations in South America is its proximity to fabled Machu Picchu, the so-called lost city of the Incas. The Spanish never found the mountaintop city, which may have been a religious retreat or a secret capital and which included a fortress, temple, and other buildings surrounded by laboriously terraced fields. Those who have visited Machu Picchu describe it as a place of breathtaking, even mystical, beauty.

The Plaza de Armas in Cuzco.

A Calendar of Peruvian Festivals

In Peru, about 3,000 festivals are celebrated annually. Many have a basis in the Christian religion or pre-Columbian traditions. The following is a sampling.

January

To usher in the **New Year**, many Peruvians eat 13 grapes for good luck.

January 6 in Peru marks the **Bajada de los Reyes** (the arrival of the Three Wise Men), the end of the Christmas season and the traditional day for exchanging gifts.

February

Puno, a highland town on the western shore of Lake Titicaca, hosts a renowned festival in honor of the **Virgen de la Candelaria** (Virgin of Candlemas). On February 2, the high point of the multi-day festival, a statue of the Virgin, Puno's patron saint, is carried through the streets. Hundreds of dance groups from neighboring towns pay their respects to the saint, wearing their finest costumes. During the following days the festivities continue with fairs, drink, and music.

Late February or early March is also the time for **Carnaval**, the celebration preceding the Catholic Lenten season. Cajamarca is particularly well known for its festivities.

March/April

In heavily Roman Catholic Peru, **Semana Santa** (Holy Week or Easter Week) is marked by public events commemorating the Passion, Crucifixion, and Resurrection of Jesus. In Ayacucho, Holy Week ceremonies are somber. On Good Friday, all the lights in the city are turned off and an image of Christ is carried through the streets on a litter filled with white roses. Townspeople wearing mourning clothes follow with lit candles. Before dawn on Easter morning, the image of Christ emerges once again from the cathedral. This time it is borne on a litter filled with white candles.

May

In the towns of Puno and Juliaca, near Lake Titicaca, May 2 marks the **Feria de las Alasitas**. During this traditional fair, people buy miniatures—houses, cars, etc.—then get the miniatures blessed. It is said that during the year, they'll get in full size what they bought in miniature.

June

The 24th of the month is the feast day of **San Juan Bautista** (St. John the Baptist). Though many towns and cities in Peru mark the occasion with a fiesta, the day is particularly important in the Amazon Basin.

June 24 is also an important day for residents of Peru's highlands. In and around Cuzco, hundreds of people reenact the ancient Inca **Inti Raymi** ritual, which paid homage to the sun god.

July

On the 15th and 16th, many places in Peru honor the **Virgen del Carmen**, considered by some

A Calendar of Peruvian Festivals

the patron saint of the mestizo population.

July 28 is **Independence Day** in Peru, commemorating the day in 1821 when José de San Martín declared the nation's independence from Spain in Lima.

August

August 15 marks the **Anniversary of Arequipa**. Civic and religious festivities in the city last a week, with various artistic and cultural activities.

On August 30, residents of San Jerónimo de Tunán celebrate the **Fiesta de San Roque**, during which they make a special effort to show hospitality to strangers.

August 30 is also the feast day of **Santa Rosa de Lima** (Saint Rose of Lima), Peru's patron saint. People with serious illnesses make pilgrimages to her shrine in downtown Lima, in search of a miracle.

October

El Señor de los Milagros (the Lord of the Miracles) is a fiesta celebrated from the 18th to the 28th throughout Peru, but especially in Lima. At the center of the festivities is the image of a black Christ, which was painted by a slave during colonial days and which survived attempts to destroy it as well as the devastating 1746 earthquake. Today the black Christ is carried through the streets of Lima in a procession that attracts tens of thousands of believers, many dressed in purple tunics.

November

On **All Saints' Day**, November 1, and **All Souls' Day**, November 2, many Peruvians attend Mass, then head to cemeteries to honor the dead.

December

Peruvians celebrate **Christmas** with music and dancing. In the capital cities of the various districts, there are competitions between Christmas carolers.

Peruvians pass **New Year's Eve** with a variety of celebrations, many of which include dancing.

Recipes

Papas a la Huancaína

(Serves 8)
10 medium potatoes (new potatoes are best)
1 pound of farmer or feta cheese
2 small hot peppers
1 cup evaporated milk
1/2 cup vegetable oil
2 cloves garlic
8 saltine crackers
1 tsp prepared mustard
Salt and pepper
Lettuce
3 hard-boiled eggs
Black olives

Directions:
1. Peel and boil potatoes. Allow to cool.
2. In a blender, blend the cheese, peppers, milk, oil, garlic, crackers, mustard, salt, and pepper. The sauce should be fairly thick. Add more crackers if not thick enough. Add more milk if too thick.
3. Lay a bed of lettuce in a serving dish and place the potatoes on top. Cover with the sauce. Cut the hard-boiled eggs in half and place on top of the potatoes. Add black olives if desired.
This dish can be served slightly cold.

Lomo Saltado

(Serves 6)
2 lbs vegetarian meat crumbles
1 tbsp red wine
2 tsp minced garlic
4 tomatoes, cut into strips
Salt and pepper
2 medium onions, cut into strips
1 bell pepper, cut into thin strips
Chopped parsley
1 tbsp vinegar
5 medium potatoes, cut into thin strips
1 tbsp oil

Directions:
1. Sauté the garlic and onion in 1 tbsp oil and wine.
2. Add the chopped tomato, salt, and pepper to the pan. Cook for a few minutes. Add the bell pepper, parsley, and vinegar. Add the vegetarian meat crumbles.
3. In a separate pan, fry the potatoes in hot oil. Add the fried potatoes to the meat. Serve with rice.

Arroz Tapado **(Covered Rice)**

(Serves 6)
3 cloves of garlic, minced
2 tbsp oil
Lemon juice
Salt
4 cups water
1 lb of washed rice
1 onion, finely chopped
2 lbs vegetarian beef crumbles
2 tomatoes, finely chopped
1 tbsp tomato paste
4 tsp raisins
5 black olives, chopped
2 hard boiled eggs, finely chopped
1 tsp parsley, chopped

Directions:
1. In a pot, sauté the garlic in oil, add a few drops of lemon juice, salt, and the water, and bring to a boil. Add the rice and continue to cook until the rice begins to dry out. Simmer, covered, until rice is done.
2. In a pan, sauté the onions. Add the vegetarian beef crumbles, tomatoes, tomato paste, raisins, olives, egg, and parsley. Mix well.
3. Coat the inside of a one-cup glass measuring cup with a little oil or shortening. Fill halfway with rice, then some of the meat filling, and finish filling with more rice. Invert onto a plate and carefully remove the measuring cup. Repeat for each serving.
Can be served cold.

Leche Asada

(Serves 8–10)
1 can of sweetened, condensed milk
1 can of evaporated milk
1 cup sugar
1 tsp vanilla extract
8 eggs, beaten
1/4 cup water

Directions:
Preheat oven to 400°F.
1. Mix the condensed milk, evaporated milk, 1/2 cup of sugar, the vanilla, and eggs.
2. In a saucepan dissolve 1/2 cup sugar in 1/4 cup of water, and heat carefully until it becomes syrupy and slightly tan.
3. Pour the caramel in a glass baking dish and pour the milk mixture on top.
4. Take a slightly larger glass dish and fill halfway with water. Place the dish with the milk mixture inside the larger dish and cover everything with aluminum foil. Cook in an oven for 30–45 minutes or until the custard is completely cooked.
Serve slightly chilled.

Glossary

arable—fit for growing crops.

arid—extremely dry.

Communist—characteristic of a political system in which workers control the means of production of goods, and private property is eliminated; or a person who supports such a system.

conquistador—a Spanish adventurer-soldier who participated in the conquest of Central and South America during the 16th century.

cordillera—a system of mountain ranges, often consisting of a number of parallel chains.

costa—Spanish word meaning "coast"; one of three natural regions in Peru.

elite—members of a privileged or ruling class.

gross domestic product (GDP)—the total value of goods and services a country produces in a one-year period.

guerrilla—a fighter engaged in irregular or unconventional warfare, especially as a member of an independent unit that practices harassment or sabotage.

indigenous—native or original to a particular area.

inflation—the increasing cost of goods and services in an economy over a period of time.

literacy—the ability to read and write.

navigable—capable of being traveled by ships and boats.

pre-Columbian—existing in, or characteristic of, the Americas before the arrival of Christopher Columbus in 1492.

rain forest—a forest that receives at least 100 inches (254 cm) of rain per year.

rural—characteristic of, or located in, the countryside.

sierra—a range of mountains, especially one with an irregular outline.

subsistence farming—farming that supplies just enough food for the farm family, with no surplus that can be sold.

temperate—having a mild or moderate climate.

terraces—fields cut into a hillside and arranged like steps.

trade winds—winds that blow almost constantly in one direction near the equator.

urban—characteristic of, or located in, a city.

Project and Report Ideas

Maps and Charts

- Using "Machu Picchu" as a search term, do a Web search for pictures of the fabled lost city of the Inca. Paste the photos on poster board and make a brief presentation to the class about the site.
- Draw a map showing the part of the world affected by El Niño. Include a paragraph on your map explaining this weather phenomenon.

Creative Writing

- Pretend that you are the first Inca to have seen the Spanish conquistadors. Describe them as someone would who has never before seen white people in armor or horses. It would be a good idea to use a picture of a 16th-century conquistador to spur your imagination.
- Pretend that you are Francisco Pizarro. Describe what you see and what you are thinking during the days before and after your encounter with Atalhuallpa at Cajamarca.

Travel Brochure

Fold a large sheet of paper in thirds, accordian-style. Label the front panel "Peru: Tourist Attractions" and include the country's flag. On the inside two panels, paste at least four photos of Peruvian sites of interest, such as Machu Picchu, Lima, and the plaza of Cajamarca. (You can get these pictures from the Internet.) Write a brief caption for each image. On the back panel, paste a map of Peru, with the locations of the tourist attractions on the inside of the brochure highlighted.

Project and Report Ideas

Web Guide

In teams, assemble a list of the best websites on Peru. Devise a rating system, and include a one- or two-sentence summary of each site. Combine the sites into a comprehensive guide to Peru for other classes to use.

Book Reports

A well-written book report can be fairly brief: one paragraph introducing the book, one paragraph summarizing its content, two paragraphs supporting opinions about the book's strengths and weaknesses, and a concluding paragraph. Choose a book about Peru and write a five-paragraph review following the format described above. Here are some good candidates:

- *Discovering the Inca Ice Maiden: My Adventures on Ampato* by Johan Reinhard.
- *Frozen Girl* by David Getz.
- *The Incas: A Novel* by Daniel Peters.
- *Temple* by Matt Reilly.
- *Chaska and the Golden Doll* by Ellen Alexander.
- *Inca: The Scarlet Fringe* by Suzanne Allés Blom.

Chronology

18,000–4,000 B.C.	Groups of Amerindians settle in Peru, eventually establishing agricultural civilizations in the region.
c. A.D. 1200	The Inca establish themselves around the highland city of Cuzco.
Early 1400s	The Inca begin conquering neighboring tribes and incorporating them into an empire; by the 16th century the Inca Empire will stretch from modern-day Colombia in the north to Chile and Argentina in the south.
1526–28	Spanish conquistador Francisco Pizarro explores Peru's coastal regions.
1532	On May 13, Pizarro, leading a group of about 180 Spanish soldiers, begins march to the interior of Peru; on November 15, the Spaniards enter Cajamarca; the following day, under the pretext of desiring a peaceful meeting, they seize the Inca emperor, Atahuallpa, and slaughter thousands of Inca warriors.
1533	After Atahuallpa has gathered a huge ransom in order to win his freedom, Pizarro has the Inca emperor executed.
1536	Manco Capac begins unsuccessful revolt against Spanish rule.
1541	Pizarro is killed by supporters of a rival conquistador he had earlier killed.
1542	Spain establishes the Viceroyalty of Peru, with Lima as its capital.
1780	An Indian revolt led by Tupac Amaru, who claimed to be descended from the last Inca chieftain, begins; it will be put down by the following year.
1821	General José de San Martín captures Lima from the Spanish and proclaims Peru independent.
1824	Battles of Junín and Ayacucho guarantee Peru's independence from Spain.
1879–83	Peru and Bolivia are defeated by Chile during the War of the Pacific; Peru loses territory in the south to Chile.

Chronology

1980	The Communist guerrilla movement *Sendero Luminoso*, or Shining Path, begins attacks against Peruvian government.
1990	Promising to end government corruption and bring the Shining Path under control, Alberto Fujimori is elected president.
1992	Fujimori suspends constitution with army backing; Shining Path's leader is arrested and sentenced to life imprisonment.
1994	Some 6,000 Shining Path guerrillas surrender to Peruvian authorities.
1995	Fujimori is elected to a second term.
2000	Amid widespread allegations of fraud, Fujimori is elected to a third presidential term, but he soon resigns following political and financial scandals; head of Congress Valentín Paniagua is sworn in as interim president.
2001	Alejandro Toledo wins presidential elections, takes oath of office to become Peru's first president of Amerindian origin.

Further Reading/Internet Resources

Falconer, Kieran. *Peru*. New York: Marshall Cavendish, 1999.

King, David C. *Peru: Lost Cities, Found Hopes*. New York: Benchmark Books, 1998.

Lyle, Garry. *Peru*. Philadelphia: Chelsea House Publishers, 1999.

Morrison, Marion. *Peru*. New York: Children's Press, 2000.

Yip, Dora, and Janet Heisey. *Welcome to Peru*. Milwaukee, Wis.: Gareth Stevens, 2002.

Travel Information

http://www.andeantravelweb.com/peru/
http://www.enjoyperu.com/
http://www.ilatintravel.com/

History and Geography

http://www.pbs.org/wgbh/nova/peru/
http://www.nationalgeographic.com/features/97/andes/
http://www.mountain.org/andes.html

Economic and Political Information

http://www.state.gov/r/pa/ei/bgn/2056.htm
http://www.dfat.gov.au/geo/peru/
http://www.economist.com/countries/Peru/

Culture and Festivals

http://www.magicperu.com/culture.htm
http://www.adventure-life.com/peru/peru_culture.html
http://www.globalanthems.com/EthnicMus/z-Esaay%201/Peruvian%20Fiestas.htm

U.S. Department of State
Bureau of Western Hemisphere Affairs
Office of Andean Affairs (Room 5906)
2201 C St., NW
Washington, DC 20520-6263
(202) 647-3360
http://www.state.gov

U.S. Department of Commerce
International Trade Administration
Office of Latin America and the Caribbean
14th St. and Constitution Ave., NW
Washington, DC 20230
(202) 482-0475
(800) USA-TRADE
http://www.ita.doc.gov

American Chamber of Commerce of Peru
Avenida Ricardo Palma 836, Miraflores
Lima 18, Peru
(511) 241-0708
E-mail: amcham@amcham.tci.net.pe
http://www.amcham.org.pe

Embassy of Peru
1700 Massachusetts Ave., NW
Washington, DC 20036
(202) 833-9860
E-mail: peru@peruemb.org
http://www.peruemb.org/main.html

Index

Index/Picture Credits

Contributors

Senior Consulting Editor **James D. Henderson** is professor of international studies at Coastal Carolina University. He is the author of *Conservative Thought in Twentieth Century Latin America: The Ideals of Laureano Gómez* (1988; Spanish edition *Las ideas de Laureano Gómez* published in 1985); *When Colombia Bled: A History of the Violence in Tolima* (1985; Spanish edition *Cuando Colombia se desangró, una historia de la Violencia en metrópoli y provincia*, 1984); and coauthor of *A Reference Guide to Latin American History* (2000) and *Ten Notable Women of Latin America* (1978).

Mr. Henderson earned a bachelor's degree in history from Centenary College of Louisiana, and a master's degree in history from the University of Arizona. He then spent three years in the Peace Corps, serving in Colombia, before earning his doctorate in Latin American history in 1972 at Texas Christian University.

Charles J. Shields is the author of 20 books for young people. He has degrees in English and history from the University of Illinois, Urbana-Champaign. Before turning to writing full time, he was chairman of the English and guidance departments at Homewood-Flossmoor High School in Flossmoor, Illinois. He lives in Homewood, a suburb of Chicago, with his wife, Guadalupe, a former elementary school principal and now an educational consultant to the Chicago Public Schools.